THE *Wonder* OF CHRISTMAS

Arranged for Women's Voices
with Accompaniment

St. Paul Books & Media

The Wonder of Christmas is also available on stereo cassette (KC008) and on compact disc (CD008).

KS008
ISBN 0-8198-8239-9

Arranged by Kurt Kaiser and William Pursell
Transcribed by William Svarda
Cover design by Edd Anthony, OFM, Franciscan Canticle, Inc.

Printed in the U.S.A.

Contents

Carol of the Bells

Peter Wilhousky

M. Leontovich
Arr. by William Pursell

9
A
pp sempre cresc.
Christ - mas is here, bring - ing good cheer to young and old, meek and the bold.
Ding, dong, ding, dong.
A
Gm
B♭/A
Cm7/E♭
Gm/B♭
mf
13
Ding, dong, ding, dong. That is their song, with joy- ful ring, all car - ol - ing.
Ding, dong, ding, dong.
Ding, dong, ding, dong.
Cm7/E♭
Gm7
Cm
Gm

17
mf
cresc.
One seems to hear words of good cheer from eve - ry- where, fill - ing the air.
One seems to hear words of good cheer from eve - ry- where, fill - ing the air.
One seems to hear words of good cheer from eve - ry- where, fill - ing the air.
Cm7/E♭
Gm7
Cm
Gm
21
B
f
cresc.
O how they pound, rais - ing the sound o'er hill and dale, tell - ing their tale.
O how they pound, rais - ing the sound o'er hill and dale, tell - ing their tale.
O, how hap - py are their tones.
B
Gm6
Gm7
Gm
f

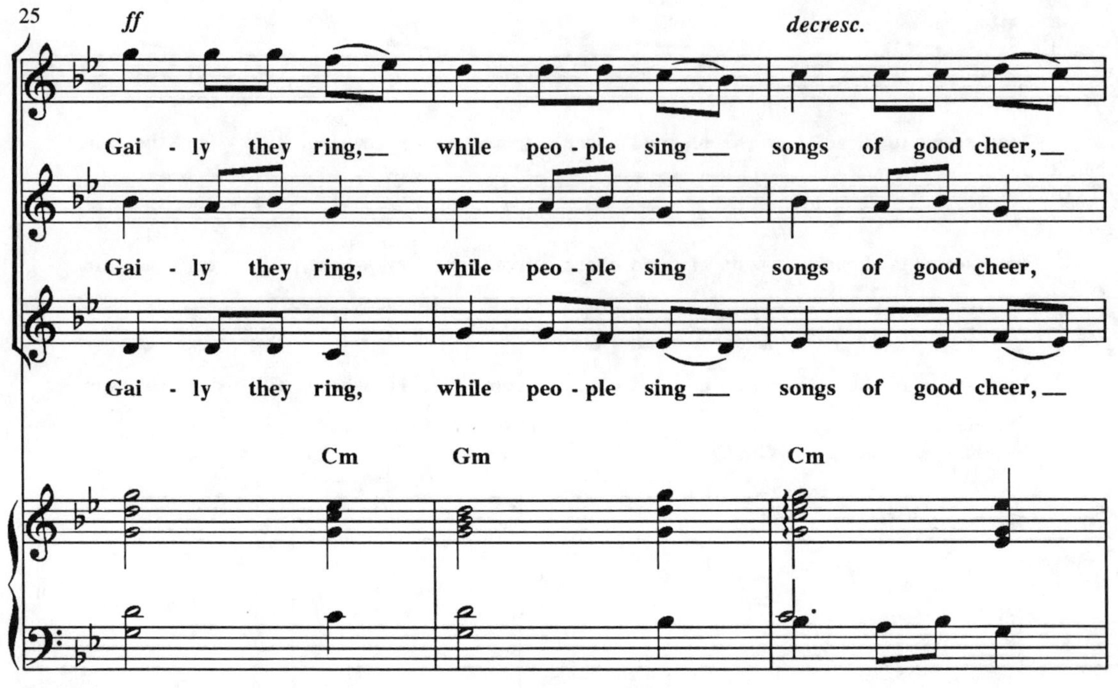
25
ff
decresc.
Gai - ly they ring, while peo - ple sing songs of good cheer,
Gai - ly they ring, while peo - ple sing songs of good cheer,
Gai - ly they ring, while peo - ple sing songs of good cheer,
Cm
Gm
Cm

28
f
Christ - mas is here! Mer - ry, mer - ry, mer - ry, mer - ry Christ - mas.
Christ - mas is here! Ding, ding, dong.
Christ - mas is here! Ding, dong, ding, dong. That is their song
Gm
Gm6
D7
Gm

31
C dim. (without rit.)
Mer - ry, mer - ry, mer - ry, mer - ry Christ - mas. On, on they send,
Ding, ding, dong. Ding,
with joy - ful ring, all car - ol - ing. Ding,
Gm6 D7 Gm C
34
1.
on with - out end their joy - ful tone to eve - ry home. Hark! How the bells,
dong, ding, dong.
dong, ding, dong,
E♭/B♭ Gm E♭/B♭ 1. Gm

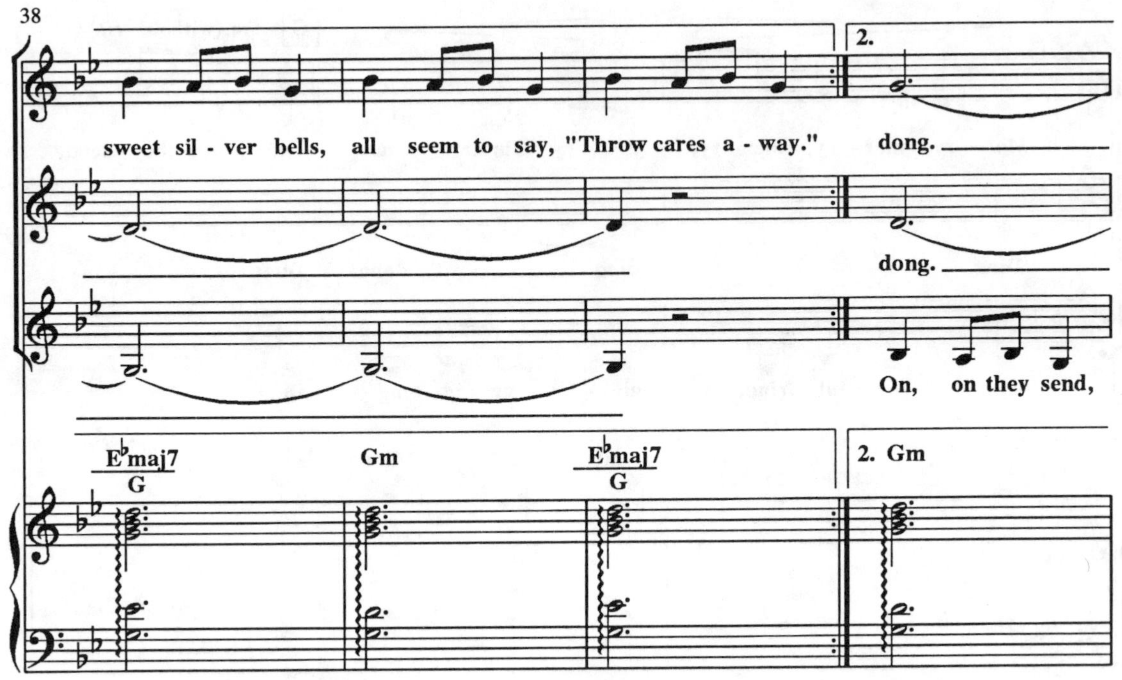
38
sweet sil - ver bells, all seem to say, "Throw cares a - way."
2.
dong.
dong.
On, on they send,
E♭maj7/G
Gm
E♭maj7/G
2. Gm

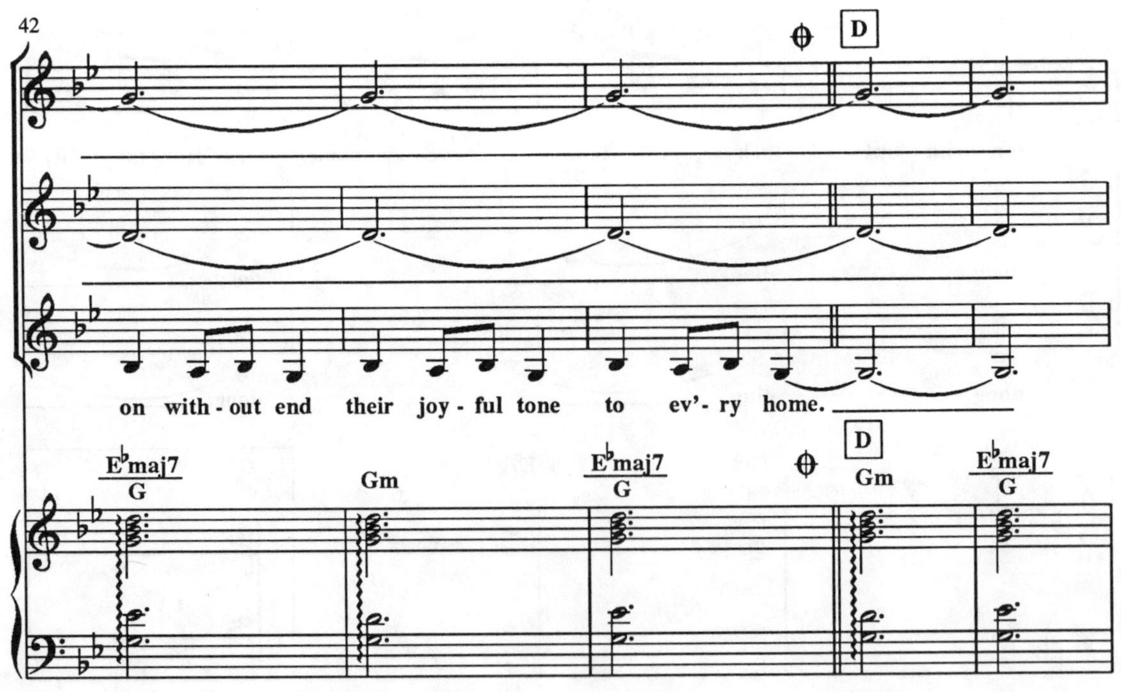
42
D
on with - out end their joy - ful tone to ev'- ry home.
E♭maj7/G
Gm
E♭maj7/G
Gm
E♭maj7/G

47
Gm
E♭/G
Gm
E♭/G
51
Gm
E♭/G
Gm
Gm6
55
Gm7
Gm
Cm/G
Gm
59
Cm/G
Gm
62
Cm7/B♭
Gm
Cm7/B♭
D.S. al ⊕
decresc.

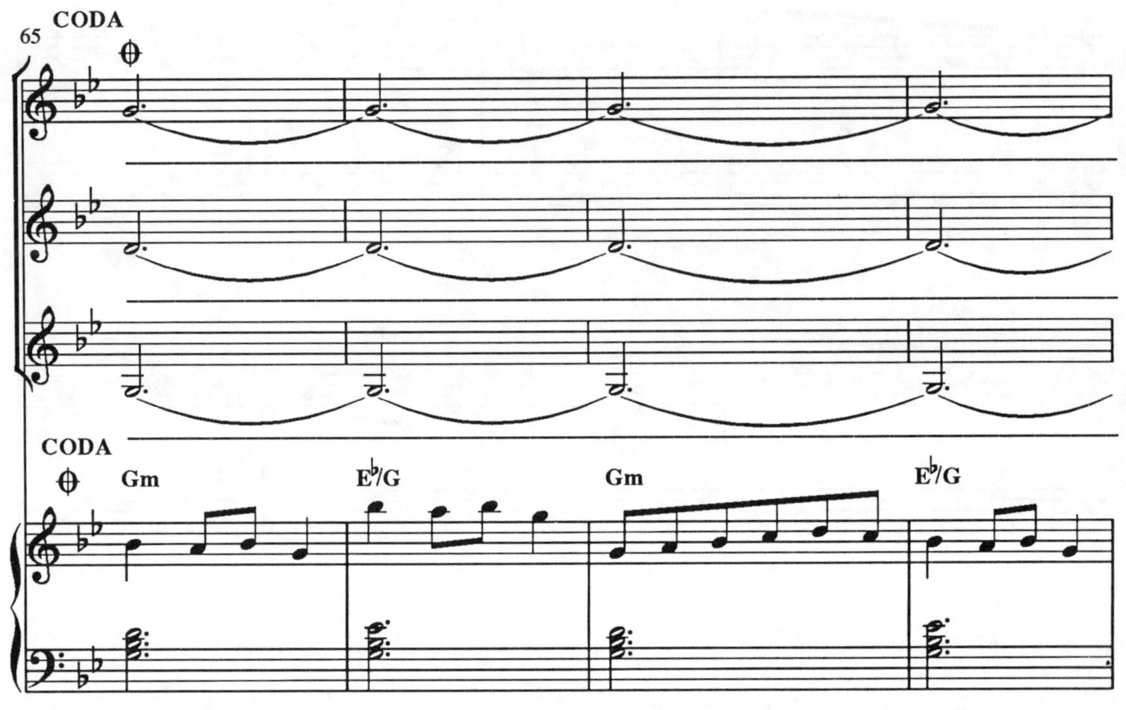

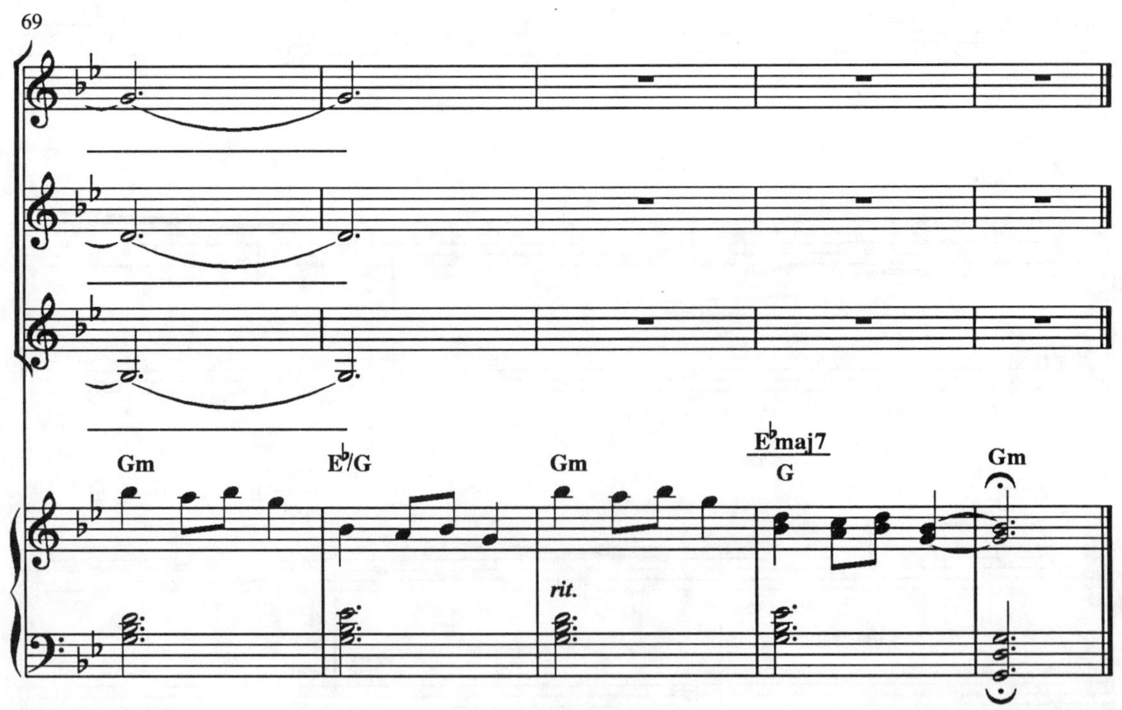

Take 1st & 2nd endings
again, then go to CODA.

O Come, All Ye Faithful

Tr. F. Oakeley

J. F. Wade
Arr. by William Pursell

12
hem. Come and__ be - hold__ him,
D G/B D/A G Dsus D G
15
born the King of an - gels, O come let us a -
D/F# B/D# Em A/C# D A D G/D D G/D D7
18
dore him, O come __ let us a - dore him, O
G/D D G/D D7 G/D D G

21
come __ let us a - dore __ him, __ Christ ______ the Lord.
D/A G/B D Asus A D/F# D/C G/B C G/D Dsus D G
mp
25
Cmaj7/G G D/G C/G D/G
28
D/F# C2/E Cmaj7/G Cmaj7
(slight rit.)
32
B
p
2. Sing choirs of an - gels. Sing __ in ex- ul - ta - tion.
B
G D/F# D G D/F# G C G/D D
p a tempo

36
Sing___ all ye cit - i - zens of heav'n___ a - bove.
Em D/F# A D A7/E D/F# G D/A A7 D
p
40
Glo - ry___ to God___ in___ the___
G/B D/A G Dsus D G D/F# B/D# Em A/C#
mp
43
high - est, O come let us a - dore him, O
D A D G/D D G/D D7 G/D
f

46
come let us a - dore him, O come let us a -
D G/D D7 G/D D G D/A G/B D Asus A
49
dore him, Christ the Lord.
D/F# D/C G/B C G/D Dsus D G
52
C
f
3. Yea Lord, we greet thee, born this hap - py
E♭7 B♭m7/E♭ E♭7 A♭ B♭m7/A♭ E♭7/A♭ A♭ E♭/G A♭ D♭
rit.
mf
a tempo

56
morn - ing. Je - sus, to thee be all glo - ry
A♭/C D♭ E♭ Fm B♭7/D E♭ B♭ E♭/G A♭ E♭/B♭ A♭/C E♭/B♭ B♭7
60
giv'n. Word of the Fa - ther,
E♭ A♭/C E♭ A♭ E♭7sus B♭ E♭7 A♭
f
63
now in flesh ap - pear - ing. O come let us a -
E♭ C Fm B♭ E♭ B♭/F E♭/G A♭/E♭ E♭ A♭/E♭ E♭7

66
dore him, O come let us a - dore him, O
A♭/E♭ E♭ A♭/E♭ E♭7 A♭/E♭ E♭ A♭
f
69
come let us a - dore him, Christ the Lord.
f
E♭/B♭ A♭/C E♭ B♭sus/F E♭/G E♭/D♭ A♭/C D♭ A♭/E♭ A♭sus/E♭ A♭
D♭maj7/A♭ A♭ E♭/A♭ D♭/A♭ E♭/A♭ E♭/G D♭2/F
73
mp
D♭maj7/A♭ D♭maj7 A♭
77
p rit.

Hush, the Baby Is Sleeping

2nd verse by
Deborah Harris

Words & Music by Kurt Kaiser
Arr. by Kurt Kaiser

13
poco rit.
qui - et - ly rest - ing his head on the hay.
A2
E/G#
F#7
B7
poco rit.
17
a tempo
See how his Moth - er is beam - ing. Her
E
Emaj7
Amaj7
F#m7
B7
E
a tempo
21
Child brings the whole world a hope - full new day.
A2
E/G#
F#7
B
B/A

25
An - gels an - nounce his birth, "Peace to all men on earth,
E Emaj7 A6 B7 C#m7 Emaj7/B
cresc.
29
glad - ly your voi - ces raise, let your hearts sing." Oh
A B/A E/G# G# C#m F#7 B B7
mf
33
hush, hush, the Ba - by is sleep - ing, tread
E Amaj7 A/G# F#m7 B7 E G#7

37
soft - ly, dear shep - herds, to hon - or your King.
Oo
Amaj7 A6 E/G♯ F♯7 B7 E
41
Amaj7 E/G♯ F♯m7 C♯m2 A B C♯m
mp
45
Hush,
F♯7 A/B B7 Emaj7
mp

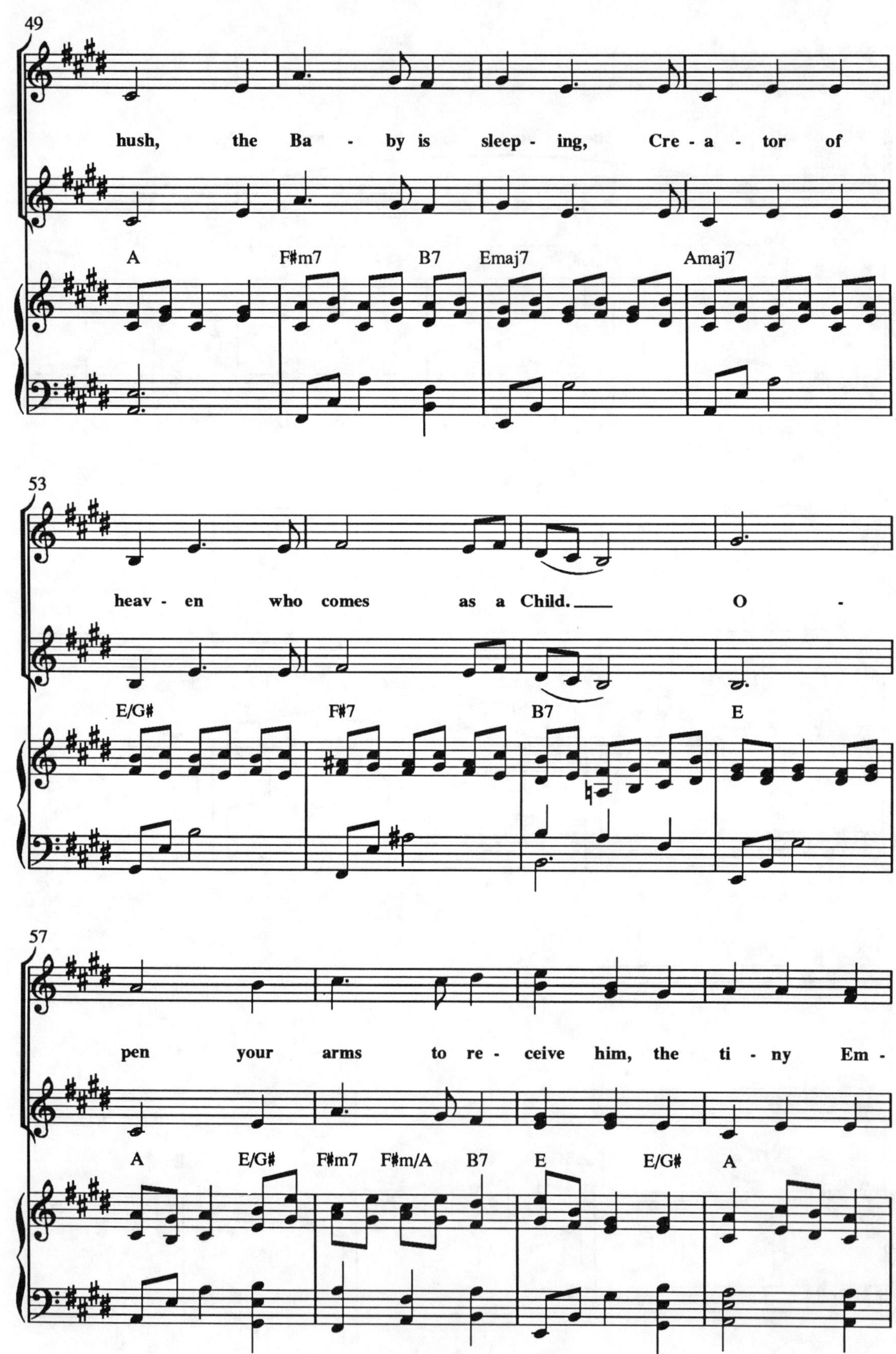
49
hush, the Ba - by is sleep - ing, Cre - a - tor of
A F#m7 B7 Emaj7 Amaj7
53
heav - en who comes as a Child.___ O -
E/G# F#7 B7 E
57
pen your arms to re - ceive him, the ti - ny Em -
A E/G# F#m7 F#m/A B7 E E/G# A

61
man - u - el___ ho - ly and mild.___ On - ly be -
E/G# E E/D# F#7 B E Emaj7/G#
65
got - ten Son, Sav - ior whose love has come in - to the
A6 G#m/B C#m F#m7 B/A
69
world and now in - to our hearts. Oh___ hush,
C#m7/G# G#m/B G#/B# C#m F#7 B B7 E
mp

73
hush, the Ba - by is sleep - ing. Qui - et - ly
A
B7
E
A
p
77
hon -
bow down and
hon - or, hon - or, hon - or,
E/G#
F#7
A2/B
81
- or your King.
hon - or your King.
B7
E
pp

Once in Royal David's City

Cecil Alexander

Henry Gaunllett
Arr. by William Pursell

10
Ba - by in a man - ger for his bed. Ma - ry
gen - tle is our Lord in heav - en a - bove. And he
Dm F/A B♭ F/C C F B♭
13
was that Moth - er mild, Je - sus Christ her lit - tle
leads his chil - dren on to the place where he is
F B♭/D C7 F B♭ F B♭ C7sus C7
16
Child.
gone.
F A Dm G/B C/B♭ F/A C/E C♯o7 Dm B♭

19
B
2. And through all his won - drous _
4. Not in that poor low - ly __
F/C
C7sus
C7
F
p
22
child - hood, he would hon - or and _ o - bey, love and
sta - ble with the ox - en stand - ing __ by, we shall
C7
F
B♭maj7
Gm7
B♭maj7
C/B♭
B♭
F/C
C
25
watch the low - ly __ maid - en, in whose gen - tle arms _ he __
see him, but _ in __ heav - en, set at God's right hand _ on __
Gm7/C
F/C
Gm7/C
C
Gm7/C
C

28
lay. Chris - tian chil - dren all must be mild, o -
high. When like stars his chil - dren crowned all in
Gm7/C
B♭2
C/D
p
31
Second time to Coda
D.S. al Coda
be - dient, good as he.
white shall wait a -
Dm7
Gm7
Csus
F
33
CODA
round.
B♭
Gm7
F2
B♭maj9
C7sus
C7
F
B♭
F/A
Gm7
F
rit.

I Saw Three Ships

Traditional English Carol
Arr. by Kurt Kaiser

8
A
1. I saw three ships come sail - ing in on Christ - mas day, on
D
A
A/D
D
(R.H.)
12
Christ - mas day. I saw three ships come sail - ing in on Christ - mas day in the
A/D
D
A/D
D
16
B
morn - ing.
2. And who was in those
A/D
D
A/D
D
B
mf
(L.H.)

20
ships all three on Christ - mas day, on Christ - mas day? And who was in those
A9
D
A/D
D
24
ships all three on Christ - mas day in the morn - ing?
Em7
D/A
A7
D
C/D
28
C
3. Our Sav - ior Christ and
G/D
D
A7/D
D
C
ff
(let ring)

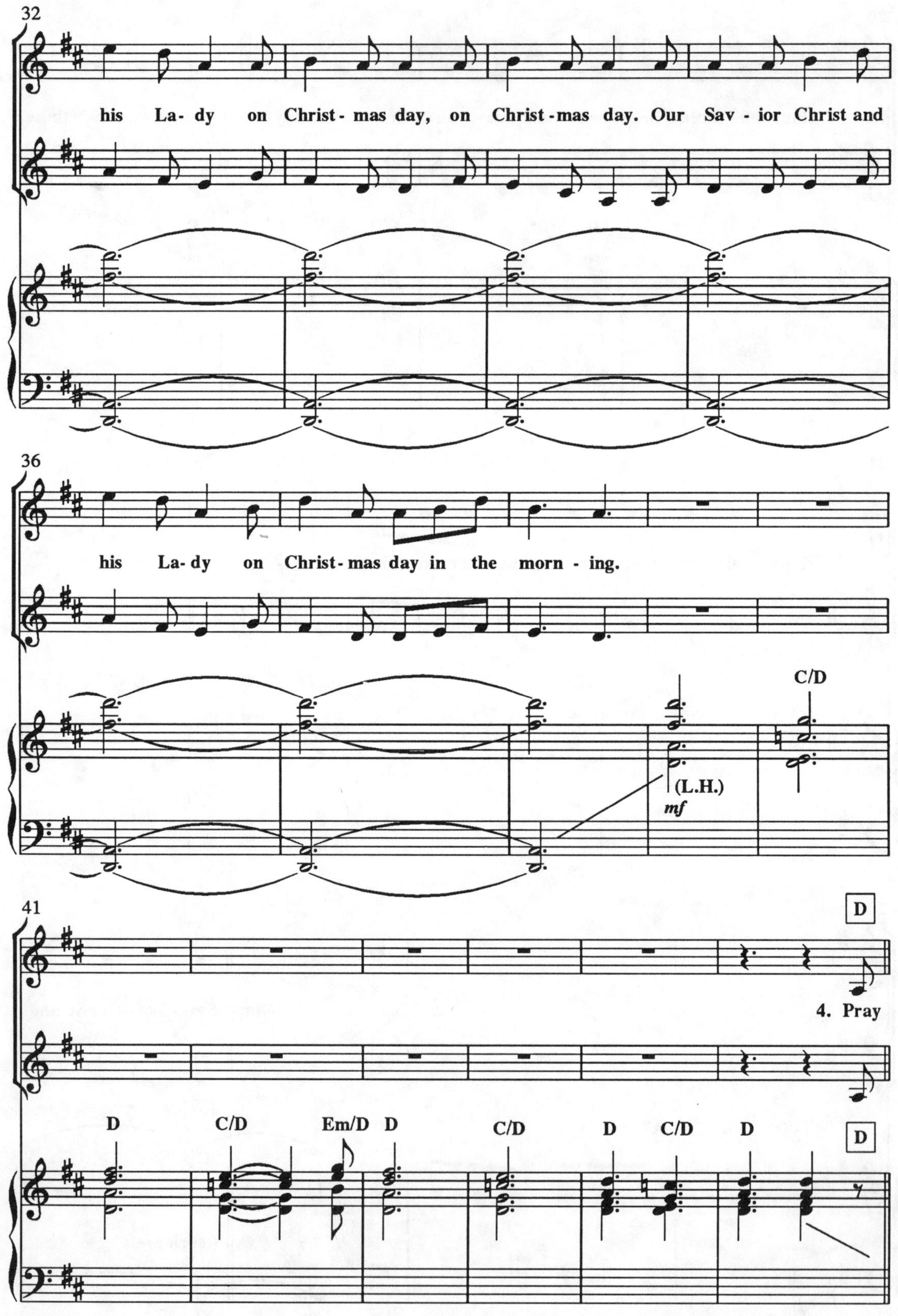
32
his La- dy on Christ - mas day, on Christ - mas day. Our Sav - ior Christ and
36
his La- dy on Christ - mas day in the morn - ing.
C/D
(L.H.)
mf
41
D
4. Pray
D
C/D
Em/D
D
C/D
D
C/D
D
D

47
whi - ther sailed those ships all three on Christ - mas day, on Christ - mas day? Pray
A
D
8va
A
f
51
whi - ther sailed those ships all three on Christ - mas day in the morn - ing?
D
G
D
8va
A
D
55
E
5. Oh they sailed in - to Beth - le - hem on
C/D
G/D
D
E
N.C.
mp

59
Christ - mas day, on Christ - mas day. Oh they sailed in - to Beth - le - hem on
63
F
Ding!
Christ - mas day in the morn - ing. 6. And all the bells on
F
D
mp
67
Dong! Ding! Dong! Ding!
earth shall ring on Christ - mas day, on Christ - mas day. And all the bells on
A7/D D A7/D D
(R.H.)

71
Dong!
Ding!
Dong!
earth shall ring on Christ - mas day in the morn - ing.
A7/D
D
Dsus
D
(R.H.)
75
pp
G
(hushed) 7. And all the an - gels of heav'n shall sing on Christ - mas day, on
G
D
Em/D
D
Em/D
D
D/F#
p
pp
79
Christ - mas day. And all the an - gels of heav'n shall sing on
Em7
Em
D
Em
D
Em/D

82
Christ - mas day in the morn - ing.
D/A
Gmaj7
B
A7
C#
D
Gmaj9
D2/F#
Em7
A6/E Em
(L.H.)
f
(slight rit.)
87
H
(broader) 8. Then let us all re - joice a - main on
A7
D2
G2
Dmaj7
G6
ff
(R.H.)
90
Christ - mas day, on Christ - mas day. Then let us all re -
D6
G2
A2
A 2 7
D
Gmaj9
(R.H.)

93
joice___ a - main on Christ - mas day in the morn - ing, in the
D7 G6 D/A A7 D
96
morn - ing, in the morn -
G6 D A7sus A7
99
ing. ___
D A2sus/F# D/A2sus D6 D

Break Forth, O Beauteous Heavenly Light

J. S. Bach
Arr. by Kurt Kaiser

13
Eb/G
Ab/C
Bb/D
Eb2
Cm
F7/A
Bb
Eb/G
p
15
Ab
Gm/Bb
Ab/C
Bb/D
Eb
Ab6
Bb7
Eb
17
Break forth, O beau - teous heav'n - ly light, and
Eb
Ab2
Bb/Ab
Eb/G
Bb/F
Cm7/Eb
F
Bb
G/B
mp
20
ush - er in the morn - ing. Ye shep - herds, shrink_ not
Ab/C
Eb
Ab/Bb
Eb/G
Fm/Ab
Bb7
Eb
Ab2
Bb/Ab
Eb/G
Bb/F

23
with af - fright, but hear the an - gel's warn - ing. This
Cm7/E♭ F B♭ G/B A♭/C E♭ B♭/A♭ E♭/G Fm/A♭ B♭7 E♭ B♭
26
Child, now weak in in - fan - cy, our con - fi - dence and
E°/G Fm D♭ B♭m6 C Fm C G/D Cm C Fm F♯°7
29
joy shall be; the pow'r of Sa - tan
Cm/G G7 Cm B♭ E♭/G Cm

31
break - ing, our peace e - ter - nal
F7/A Bb Eb/G Ab Gm/Bb Ab/C Bb/D Eb
33
mak - ing. This Child, now weak in
Ab6 Bb7 Eb Bb/Eb Eb Bb Fm C/G Fm Db
f
mp
36
in - fan - cy, our con - fi - dence and joy shall be; the
G7(b5)/B C2 Fm C2 G/D Cm/Eb C/E Fm F#o7 Cm/G G7 Cm Bb
cresc.

39
pp
pow'r of Sa - tan break - ing, our
Eb/G Eb Ab/C Bb/D Eb2 Cm F7/A Bb Eb/G
f
pp
41
peace e - ter - nal ___ mak - ing.
Ab Gm/Bb Ab/C Bb/D Eb Ab6 Bb7 Eb

Caroling, Caroling

Wihla Hutson

Alfred Burt
Arr. by William Pursell

15
Car - o - ling, car - o - ling through the snow, Christ - mas bells are ring - ing!
Dm7 G2 Dm7 G2 C7sus C F/A C7/G F
19
Joy - ous voi - ces sweet and clear sing the sad of heart to cheer.
Cm B♭/D Cm/E♭ C7/E F C7 F B♭/D Cm/E♭ B♭/F F#°7 Gm D7 Gm
f
23
Ding! Dong! Ding! Dong! Christ - mas bells are ring - ing!
E♭ B♭/D F7/C B♭ Cm/E♭ B♭/D Cm F7 F7/B♭
ff

Cm
B°
Cm/E♭
C7/E
F
C7
F
B♭/D
Cm/E♭
B♭/F
F♯°7
Gm
D7
Gm
E♭
B♭/D
F7/C
B♭
Cm/E♭
B♭/D
Cm
F7
F7/B♭
B♭
E♭/F
B♭
E♭/F
B
mp
Car - o - ling, car - o - ling through the town, Christ - mas bells are ring - ing!
B
B♭
Dm
B♭
Dm
E♭/B♭
B♭
Gm
p

41
Car - o - ling, car - o - ling up and down, Christ - mas bells are ring - ing!
Dm G Dm C7sus C7 E♭/F F
45
Mark ye well the song we sing. Glad - some tid - ings now we bring.
Cm B♭/D Cm/E♭ C7/E F C7/G F B♭/D Cm/E♭ B♭/F F♯°7 Gm D7 Gm
49
Ding! Dong! Ding! Dong! Christ - mas bells are ring - ing!
E♭ B♭/D F7/C B♭ Cm/E♭ B♭/D Cm F7 F7/B♭ B♭
f

53
B♭
E♭/F
B♭
E♭2
C
F/G
C
F/G
G7/B
57
C
Car - o - ling, car - o - ling near and far, Christ - mas bells are ring - ing!
C
C
Em7
C
Em7
F
Em7
Dm7
G7
C
Am
61
Fol - low - ing, fol - low - ing yon - der star, Christ - mas bells are ring - ing!
Em7
A2
Em7
A2
C/D
D
G/B
D7/A
G

65
ff
Sing we all this hap - py morn, "Lo, the King of heav'n is born!" Ding! Dong!
Dm Em Dm/F D7/F# G D7/A G C/E Dm/F C/G G#°7 Am F C/E
ff
70
Ding!
Ding! Dong! Christ- mas bells are ring - ing!
Dong!
Ding!
G7/D C Dm/F C/E Dm G7 C2sus C/E C2
Ding!
Ding!
75
Dong!
Ding!
Ding!
Ding!
Dong!
f

Go, Tell It on the Mountain

American Folk Song
Arr. by Kurt Kaiser

7
moun - tain, ov - er ___ the hills and ev' - ry - where. ___
Am7 Dm C7 F B♭ C
10
Go, tell it on the moun - tain that Je - sus Christ ___ is
F B♭ F/A Dm B♭6 F/C C7
13
born. Go, tell it on the moun - tain,
F B♭/C F B♭/F F F/A
f

16
ov - er ___ the hills and ev' - ry - where. ___ Go, tell it on the
C7 F B♭ C F B♭
19
moun - tain that Je - sus Christ ___ is
F/A Dm7 Gm7 Gm7/C C7
21
1. While shep - herds kept their watch - ing o'er
2. The shep - herds feared and trem - bled when
3. Down in a low - ly man - ger the
born.
F Gm7 Am Dm7

24
B♭6 Gm7/C C7 F Dm C/B♭ F/A Dm
1. si - lent flocks by night, be - hold through - out the heav - ens there
2. lo, a - bove the earth rang out the an - gel cho - rus that
3. hum - ble Christ was born; and brought us God's sal - va - tion that
28
G7 F/G G7 rall.
1. 2.
C C9
3.
C C9
1. shone a ho - ly light.
2. hailed the Sav - ior's birth.
3. bless - ed Christ - mas morn.
1. 2.
3.
rall.
rall.
31
Go, tell it on the moun - tain, o - ver the hills and
Go, tell it on the moun - tain, o ver the hills and
F B♭maj7 F C B♭ C
f a tempo

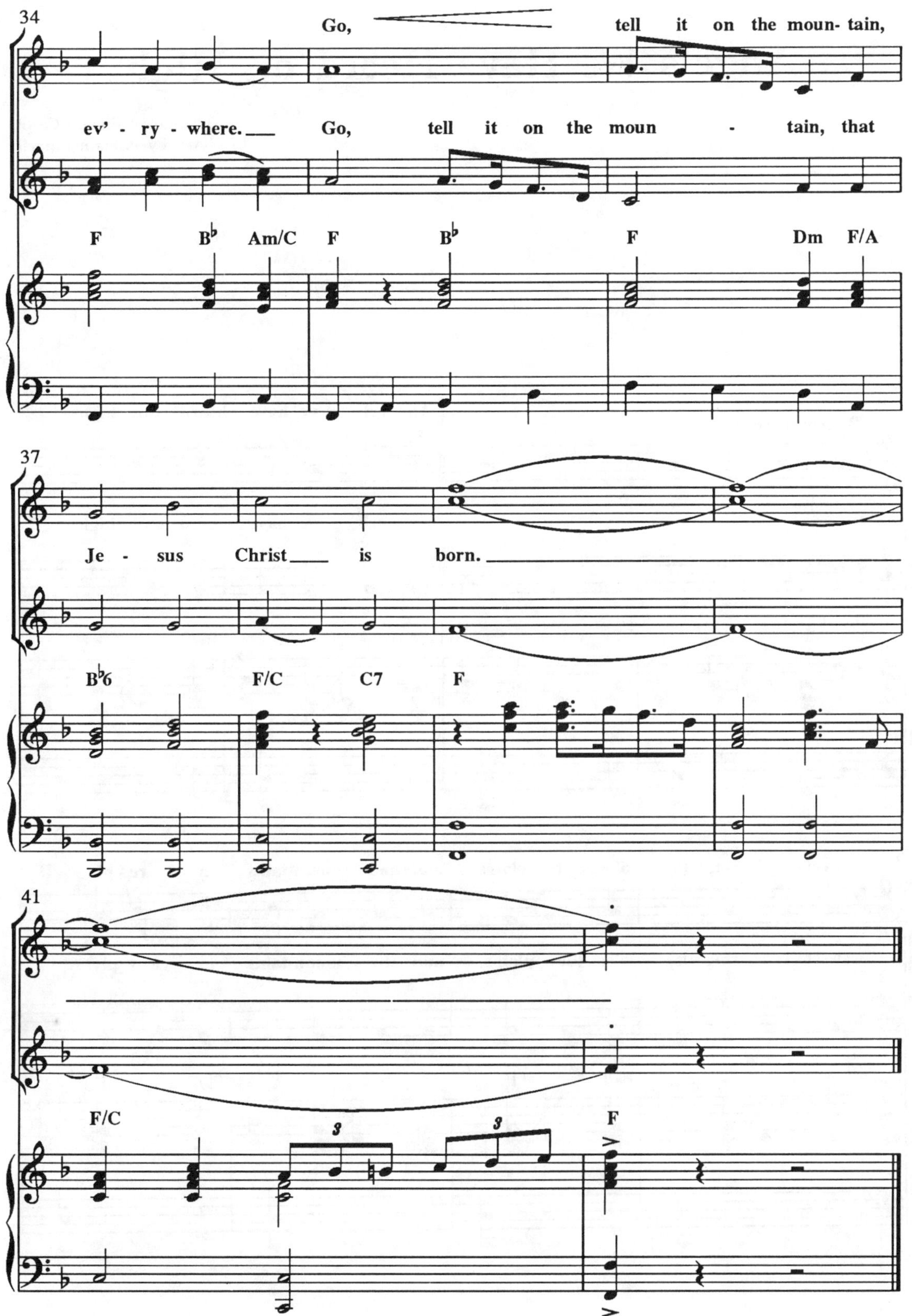
34
Go, tell it on the moun- tain,
ev' - ry - where. Go, tell it on the moun - tain, that
F B♭ Am/C F B♭ F Dm F/A
37
Je - sus Christ is born.
B♭6 F/C C7 F
41
F/C F

Angels We Have Heard on High

Traditional French Carol
Arr. by William Pursell

ech - o - ing their joy - ous strains.
B
Glo
mf
echo - ing their joy - ous strains. Glo - ri - a, glo - ri - a,
B♭/F C/F F F D7 Gm7 C7
13
ri - a
glo - ri - a, glo - ri - a in ex - cel - sis De - o!
Fmaj7 B♭ C/E B♭/D C C/B♭ F/A C F B♭ F/C C
cresc.
17
Glo - ri - a.
Glo - ri - a, glo - ri - a, glo - ri - a, glo ri - a.
Am Dm7 Gm7 C Gm7 B♭ C/E B♭/D C7 C/B♭
decresc.

21
Second time to
In ex - cel - sis De - o!
F/A C F B♭ F/C
Second time to
C
F
p
25
C
Come to Beth-le - hem and see him whose birth the an - gels sing;
Come to Beth-le - hem and see him whose birth the an-gels sing;
C
F
N.C.
p
29
Come a - dore on bend - ed knee Christ the Lord, the new-born King.
Come a - dore on bend-ed knee Christ the Lord,_the new-born King.

33
Glo - - - ri - a
Glo - ri - a, glo - ri - a, glo - ri - a, glo ri - a
D
F D7 Gm7 C7 Fmaj7 B♭ C/E B♭/D C7 C/B♭
37
Glo - -
in ex - cel - sis De - o! Glo - ri - a, glo - ri - a,
F/A C F B♭ F/C C Am7 Dm7 Gm7 C C7
p
41
ri - a
glo - ri - a, glo ri - a In ex - cel - sis De -
Fmaj7 B♭ C/E B♭/D C C/B♭ F/A C F B♭ F/C C

45
o!
F
D7
Gm7
C
Fmaj7
B♭
C/E B♭/D
C C/B♭
f
49
F/A
C/B♭
F
B♭
F/C
C
Am7
Dm
Gm7
C
mp
53
Am7
Dm7
Gm7
C7
F/A
C
F
B♭
F/C
Csus
C
57
E
p (smoothly)
mf
See with - in a man - ger laid
F
E
B♭/F
F
p

61
Je - sus, Lord of heav'n and earth.
p
Je - sus, Lord of heav'n and earth. Ma - ry, Jo - seph,
B♭/F
F
64
mf
D.S. al Coda
Sav - ior's birth.
lend your aid, with us sing our Sav - ior's birth.
B♭/F
F
B♭/F
C/F
F
67
CODA
rit.
o!
F
p
decresc.
rit.
pp

O Little Town of Bethlehem

Phillips Brooks

Traditional English
Arr. by Kurt Kaiser

13
by; yet in thy dark street shi - neth the
G
Em2
Cmaj7
E
D6
Am7
C
Bm7
mf
17
ev - er - last - ing light. The hopes and fears of all the years are
Em7
A2
D
G
C
D/C
G/B
C
Em9
21
met in thee to - night.
Am7
G/B
C6
D7
G
Am7
G/B
C6
Dm7
E7
Am
mf
p

25
Solo
O morn- ing stars, to - geth - er pro -
Oo
A6 G+ C6 D7 G Am7/G Gmaj7 G6
mf
(L.H.)
p
29
claim the ho - ly birth, and prais - es sing to God the King and
Oo
F/A G7/B C6 D7 G Am7/G Gmaj7 G6

33
peace to ___ men on earth. For ___ Christ is born ___ of ___ Ma - ry, and
Oo
F/A G7/B C6 D7 G D Em Bm
37
gath - ered all a - bove, while mor - tals sleep the an - gels ___ keep their
Oo
Em A D G Am7/G Gmaj7 G6 Dm7 G7

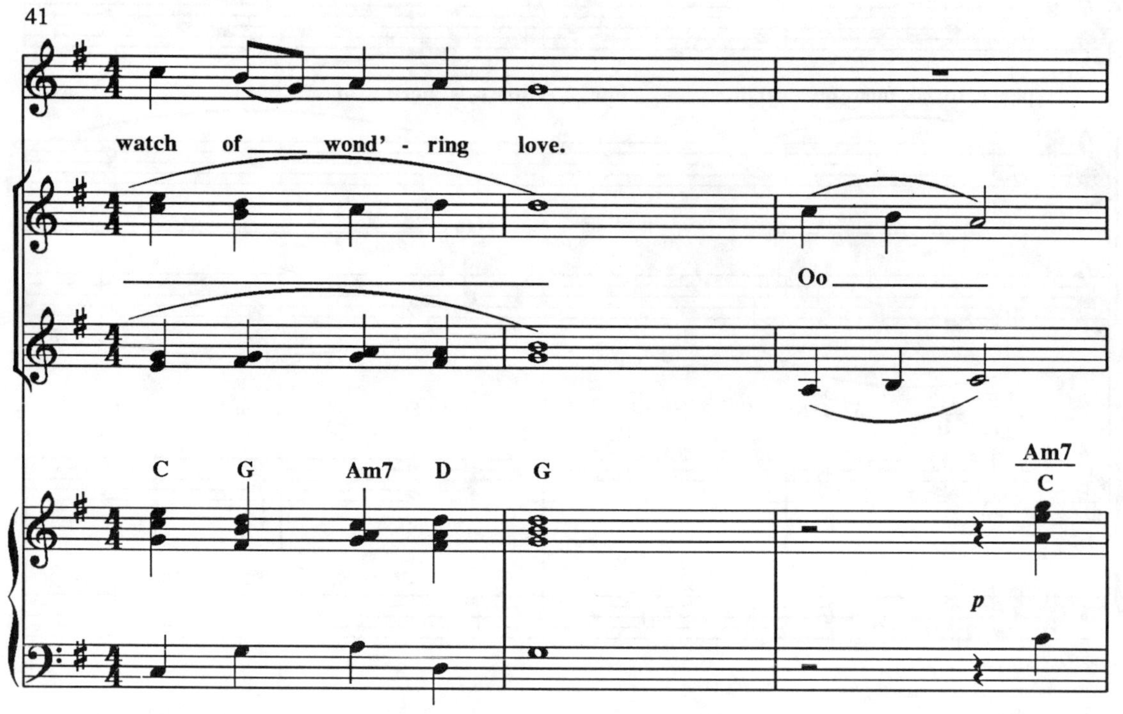
41
watch of wond' - ring love.
Oo
C G Am7 D G
Am7/C
p

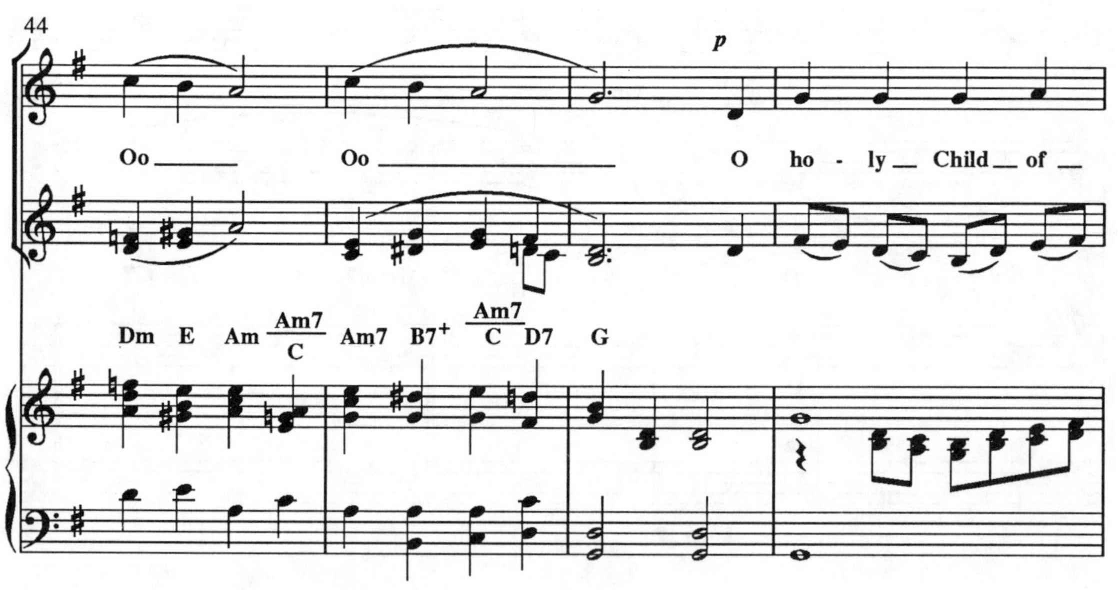
44
p
Oo
Oo
O ho - ly Child of
Dm E Am Am7/C Am7 B7+ Am7/C D7 G

48
Beth - le - hem, de - scend on us to - day. Cast
Am7 G/B C6 D G C/G G
51
out our sin and enter in, be born in us to -
Am7 G/B C6 D
54
day. We hear the Christ - mas an - gels, the
We hear the
G C/G G C6/G D/F# D Em C Bm Am(sus) D7/A

57
great glad tid - ings tell. O come to us, a -
G/B A/C♯ A7/C♯ D Bm/C Am/C G/B G Am/C D
60
bide with us, our Lord Em - man - u - el.
Em7 C G/B Em C Em C6 D G Am/G G
63
rit.
Come to us, a - bide with us, Lord Em - man - u - el.
D7/A G+/B C6 Dm7 E Am D7/A G/B C6 D G
rit.

Do You Hear What I Hear?

Noel Regney and Gloria Shayne
Arr. by William Pursell

8
Do you see what I see?
Way up in the sky, lit - tle lamb.
F/C C F/G G C Gm7 C
11
pp
Do you see what I see? Oo
Do you see what I see? A star, a star,
F/G C F/C C G7sus C Am
14
with a
dan-cing in the night with a tail as big as a kite,
Em F G F E

17
tail as big as a kite."
2. Said the
F C/E Dm7 G7 C Gm7 C
20
B
lit - tle lamb to the shep- herd boy,
"Do you hear what I hear?
B
Gm7 C F/G C
p
23
Do you hear what I hear?
Ring- ing through the sky, shep - herd boy.
F/C C F/G G C Gm7 C

26
Oo
Do you hear what I hear?
Oo
Do you hear what I hear?
A song, a song,
F/G C F/C C G7sus C Am
29
with a voice as big as the sea, with a
high a - bove the tree
Em F G F E
32
voice as big as the sea."
3. Said the
F C/E Dm7 G7 C Gm7 C
mf

35
C
shep- herd boy to the might- y king,
"Do you know what I know? ___
Do you know what
C
Gm7 C
C C/B F/A C/G
38
Do you know what I know?
In your pal- ace warm, might - y king.
I know?
C C/B F/A C/G C Gm7 C
41
Do you know what I know? A child, a
Do you know what I know?___ A child, a child,
Do you know what I know?
C/B F/A C/G C C/B F/A C/G Am

44
child, let us bring him sil - ver and gold, let us
shi - vers in the cold, let us bring him sil - ver and gold,
Em F G F E
47
bring him sil - ver and gold."
F C/E Dm7 G7 C Gm7 C
50
D
f
4. Said the king to the peo - ple ev - ery -
D♭ A♭m7 D♭ D A♭m7
f

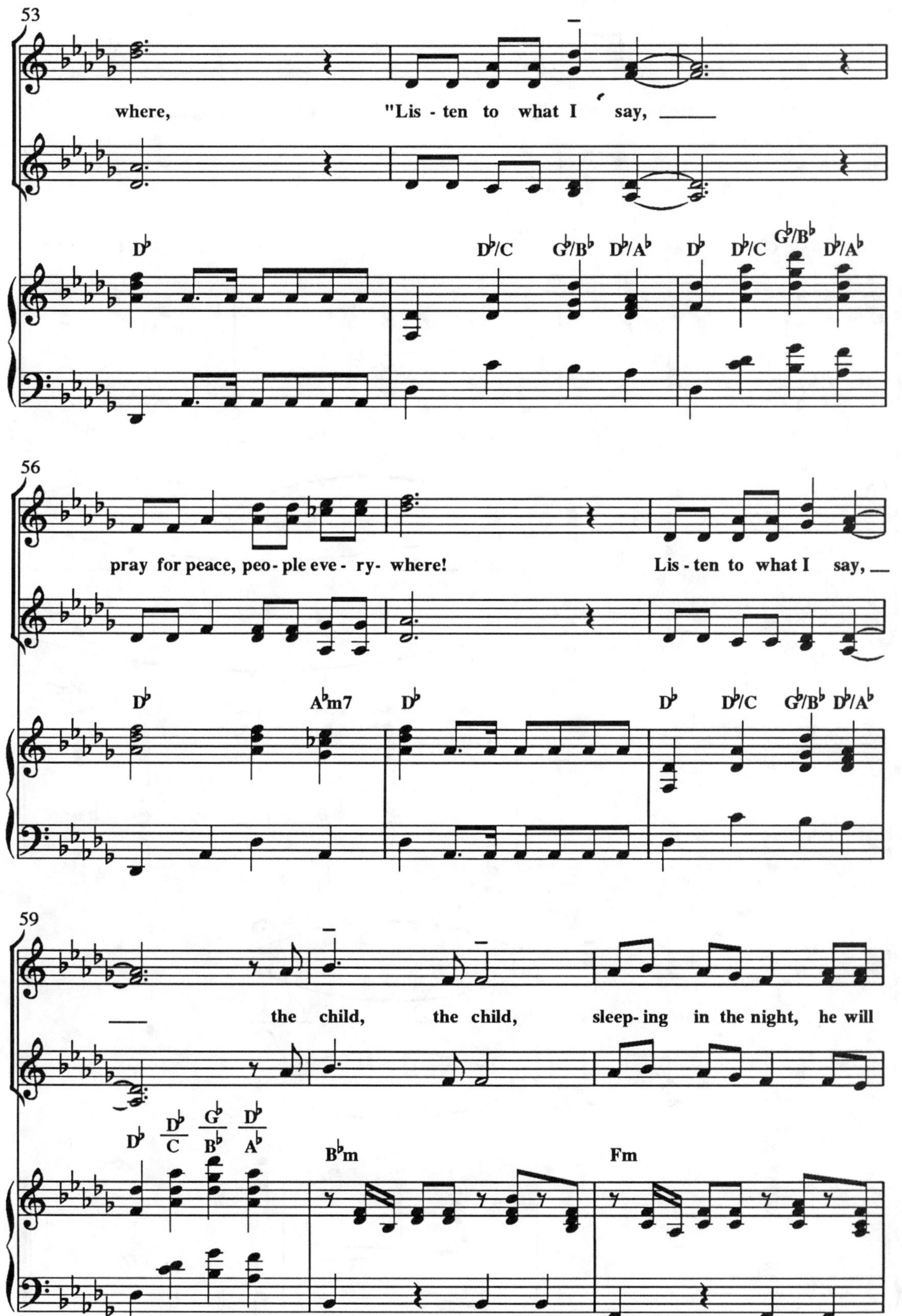
53
where, "Lis - ten to what I say,
D♭ D♭/C G♭/B♭ D♭/A♭ D♭ D♭/C G♭/B♭ D♭/A♭
56
pray for peace, peo - ple eve - ry - where! Lis - ten to what I say,
D♭ A♭m7 D♭ D♭ D♭/C G♭/B♭ D♭/A♭
59
the child, the child, sleep - ing in the night, he will
D♭ D♭/C G♭/B♭ D♭/A♭ B♭m Fm

62
bring us good - ness and light,
he will bring us
G♭ A♭ G♭ F B♭m D♭/A♭ G♭ D♭/F
65
good - ness and light,
E♭m7 A♭7 D♭ A♭m7 D♭ A♭m7
68
bring us light!"
D♭
8va

In the Bleak Midwinter

Christina Rossetti

Harold Darke
Arr. by Kurt Kaiser

13
F
F7/A
B♭2
Gm
Snow had fal - len, snow on snow, snow on
cresc.
C7sus
D
C7
E
16
C
F
B♭2
F/C
snow. In the bleak mid - win - ter long
decresc.
20
C
F
B♭maj7
a - go.
decresc.
24
Dm
C/D
Dm
C/D
B♭
Gm7/D
E - nough for him whom che - ru - bim wor - ship night and
mp

28
F C7/G F/A Am7 Gm7/B♭ Dm9 Gm7 F/A
day, a heart ___ full of mirth and a man - ger full of
32
Gm7/B♭ C7 F F7/A B♭ Gm
hay. E - nough for him whom an - gels fall down be -
36
C7/E C7 F Fmaj7 B♭ F/C
fore, the ox and ass and cam - el, which a - dore. ___
40
B♭/C C C7sus
mp
pp

43
(Solo)
What can I give him, poor as I am?
(Chorus)
Oo
Oo
F C/E Dm Am/C B♭ Gm7/D F C7/G
p
47
If I were a shep - herd, I would bring a lamb.
Oo
Oo
F/A B♭ Dm7 Gm7 Am7 B♭ C7
51
If I were a wise man, I would do my part. Yet,
F2 F7 B♭2 Gm7 C

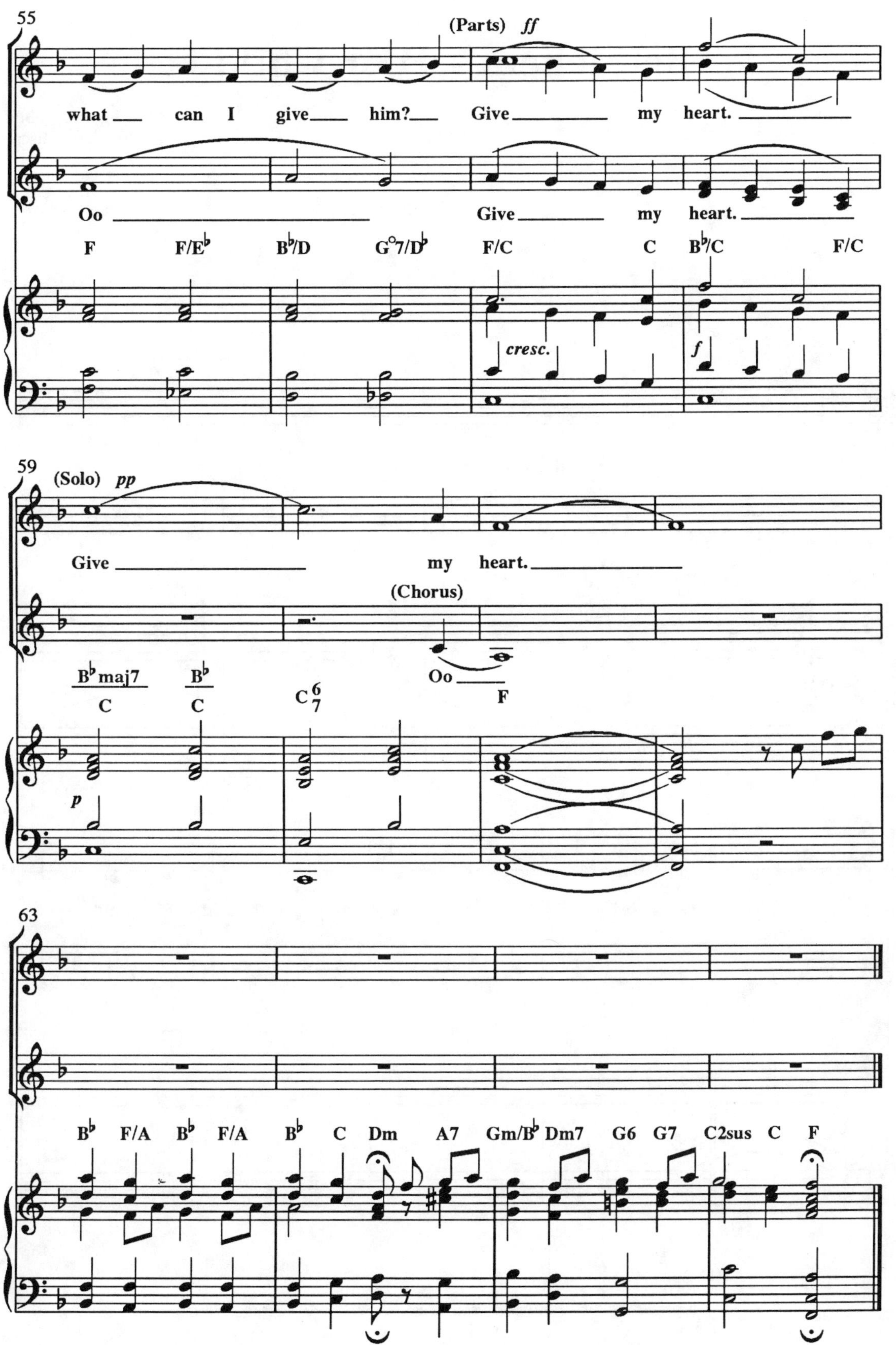

55
(Parts) ff
what can I give him? Give my heart.
Oo Give my heart.
F F/E♭ B♭/D G°7/D♭ F/C C B♭/C F/C
cresc.
f
59
(Solo) pp
Give my heart.
(Chorus)
Oo
B♭maj7/C B♭/C C 6 7 F
p
63
B♭ F/A B♭ F/A B♭ C Dm A7 Gm/B♭ Dm7 G6 G7 C2sus C F

Bethlehem's Poor Child

Melissa Wright

Sr. Janet Peter Figurant, FSP
Arr. by Kurt Kaiser

10
that very - y mo - ment the Word took on flesh. He's born in a
Am Dm7 G7 C2
15
man - ger with cat - tle to greet him. The an - gels a - dore him. Come,
Em E7 Am Cmaj7/G Dm/F C/E Gm/F Fm C/G
20
give him your gift.
What can I
Dm7/G G7 C2 F C F

26
give him, the Lord of cre - a - tion? If I had a pal - ace __ to
C/E G7 C2 Fmaj7 G7/F C/E G/B
31
of - fer to him, I'm sure he would rath - er re - main in his
C C/E G Dm7 G/F C/E G Am/G G
36
man - ger. The King of the heav - ens __ is poor - er than I.
C C7/E F2 Dm/F Dm7 Dm9/G G7 C

41
He reigns with-out fan-fare in Beth-le-hem's
C G/B Am Dm7/F Dm7 G
46
squal-or, with shep-herds as cour-tiers, no scep-ter, no
C2 Fmaj7 Em F Dm7
50
crown. Yet kings pay him hom-age, and they say as I do:
G G/F C/E F F/C C C G/B E7 Am

55
"Beth - le - hem's poor child is rich - er than I."
Fm6
C2/E
Dm7
G
G7
C
(L.H.)
60
He does not seek rich - es or emp - ty pre - ten - tion. His
Asus
A
D
A/D
G/D
D
F#
f
66
name and his glo - ry are high a - bove __ these. But __ hearts that are
Bm
F#m/A
G
Em7
A
D

71
ea - ger to love with- out meas- ure, to Beth - le - hem's poor child are
Bm/F#
Dmaj7/A
F#/A#
Bm
E°7/G
D/F#
Em7/G
D/A
F#/A#
Bm
76
pre - sents of gold.
Oo
Em7
A
D
D7
G
Dsus/A
D/A
G
A
D
p
rit.
82
Gmaj7/D
D
pp

Joy to the World

Isaac Watts

George F. Handel
Arr. by William Pursell

11
And
ev' - ry heart pre - pare him room.
15
heav'n and na - ture sing, and heav'n and na - ture sing, and
And heav'n and na - ture sing, and heav'n and na - ture
A
A7
mp
19
heav - en!
And heav - en and na - ture sing!
sing!
D D/F♯
G
D A7/E D/F♯ G6
D A D
f

23
A7
D/A
A
Em7/A
28
SOLO
B
Joy to the world! The Sav - ior reigns. Let
B
D
G
D/A
A7
D

33
men their songs em - ploy
while fields and
G
A
D
mp
38
floods, rocks, hills, and plains, re -

41
peat the sound - ing joy, re - peat the sound - ing
f
re - peat the sound- ing joy, re -
Gmaj9/A D6,9/A Gmaj9/A D6,9/A G/A A9
44
joy, re - peat, re - peat the sound - ing
peat the sound - ing joy!
G/A A9 D A/E D G/A D G D/A A7

a tempo
48
rit.
C
joy!
He rules the world with truth and
f
He rules the world with truth and
D Bm7 Bb7sus Bb7 Eb Ab/Eb Eb Ab Eb/Bb Bb7sus Bb7
C
rit.
f
a tempo
53
grace, and makes the na - tions prove the
grace, and makes the na - tions prove
Eb Ab Bb Eb Bb

58
glo - ries ___ of ___ His right - eous - ness, ___ And
Ding! Dong! Ding! Dong! Ding! Dong! Ding! Dong!
E♭/B♭ B♭7sus E♭sus E♭/B♭ B♭7sus E♭sus

62
won - ders of His ___ love, and ___ won - ders of His ___
mp
And won - ders of His ___ love, and
E♭ B♭
mp

65
love, and wonders and won - ders
won - ders of his love, and won - ders
B♭7 E♭ E♭/G A♭ E♭ B♭/F E♭/G A♭6
f
68
of his love!
of his love!
E♭/B♭ B♭7sus B♭7 E♭

Silent Night

9
'round yon Vir - gin, Moth-er and Child, ho - ly in - fant so ten - der and mild,
Fmaj7 Dm7 Am7 Cmaj7/G Fmaj7 Dm7 G A7sus Am
13
sleep in heav - en-ly peace, sleep in heav - en-ly peace.
pp
Oo
F G9 Am7 D9 C/G F/G G7 C F/G

17
B
— 2. Si - lent night, ho - ly night! Shep-herds quake
Oo Oo Oo Oo
C F/G B C Fmaj7/G C C6 F6/G G7
21
at the sight! Glo - ries stream from heav-en a - far, heav'n-ly hosts sing
p
Oo Ah Ah Ah
p
C Fmaj7 F6 Am7 C/G Fmaj7 Dm7

25
al - le - lu - ia. Christ the Sav - ior is born, Christ the Sav-ior is
pp
Ah Al - le - lu - ia. Al - le - lu - ia.
pp
Em G/A Am F6 F/G G7 Am D9 C/G F/G G7
29
C
born. Si - lent night, ho - ly night!
Si - lent night, ho - ly
Oo Oo
C F/G C F/G C C Fma7/G C C6

33
Son of God, love's pure light ra-diant beams from thy ho - ly face,
night! Son of God, Al - le-lu - ia. le - lu - ia. Al - le-lu -
Ah Ah Ah
Ah
F6/G G7 C Fmaj7 F6 Am7 C/G
37
with the dawn of re - deem - ing grace. Je - sus Lord, at thy
ia. le - lu - ia. Je - sus Lord, at thy
Ah Ah Je - sus Lord, at thy
Fmaj7 Dm7 Em G/A Am F6 F/G G7

40
Lord, at thy birth!
rit.
a tempo
birth, Je - sus Lord, at thy birth! Al - le - lu -
birth, Je - sus Lord, at thy Al - le - lu - ia.
birth, Je - sus Lord, at thy birth!
Am D9 C/G F/G G7 C Fmaj7
rit.
a tempo
44
rit.
ia. Al - le - lu - ia.
Al - le - lu - ia. Al - le - lu - ia.
Al - le - lu - ia. Al - le - lu - ia.
Al - le - lu - ia. Al - le - lu - ia.
C Fmaj7 C Fmaj7 C Fmaj7 C
simile
rit.